Wilfried Kriese
Otto E. Rössler

ENCOURAGING TO REALISE LAMPSACUS

The MULICULTURAL SOCIETY OF MINORITIES
The Internet as Chance

for our children

Impressum
Wilfried Kriese/Otto E. Rössler
COURAGE TO REALISE
LAMPSACUS
The MULICULTURAL SOCIETY OF MINORITIES
The Internet as Chance
Front cover Wilfried Kriese
Edition Wilfried Kriese 2017
First edition 1998

© 2022, Mauer Verlag
ISBN: 9783868124934

ABOUT THE BOOK
Do you want to help us
that we are no longer
regarded as dreamers,
although we might
be dreamers?

Inhalt

PREFACE

The authors are no computer experts but simply computer users trying to cope with the nearly perfect chaos of the computer world. In the meantime this also included the Internet. The computer and everything around it increasingly has become the centre of our life. For one of the authors, Otto Rössler, the chaos in the computer constitutes a vital part of his research activities. For the other author, Wilfried Kriese, the computer with its programmes has become an indispensable aid, as it makes so many book projects possible, which would not have been realisable in 1985 neither in technical nor in economic terms. The computer is the salvation particularly for the writer Wilfried Kriese, because - due to his dyslexia - he and many other people with the same disorder would not stand a chance to keep pace with today's time if it were not for computers.

In 1989 Wilfried Kriese wrote his first book on a type-writer with an alphameric storage and a spell checker which was a great help despite the underdeveloped technology of that time. Today Kriese's life that is determined by writing and publishing would be unthinkable without computers. For a person with dyslexia the computer thus became what a white stick and guide-dog are for a blind person.

For the authors there is no doubt that the Internet will make its entrance in the next 10 or 20 years even among those people who are still fighting tooth and nail to prevent the progress of the Internet or who are not able to afford it. This does not mean that it would not be worthwhile to be sceptical. This book intends to encourage you in a critical spirit to become a co-creator of the world inside and outside the Internet.

6

For the Internet will strongly influence the culture and tradition of all countries, it may even lead to a new global culture.

Lampsacus is a means to bring together the world and to unite it to a "multicultural society of minorities".

Part I LAMPSACUS

WHAT IS LAMPSACUS?

Lampsacus was an ancient Greek city that became famous because it granted asylum to the Presocratic naturalist Anaxagoras, after he had postulated the idea that the chaos was controlled by the mind as explanation for the world and consequently had been outlawed in Athens. Thus both Anaxagoras and the inhabitants of Lampsacus became immortal.

At present, there is little trust throughout the world - as was the case in the past - that science might attain transparency of the world down to the infinitely small level, as Anaxagoras was the first to propose. For this reason persons seeing the future optimistically once again need a place of refuge. Accordingly, it has the name Lampsacus. Everybody can visit this place. Lampsacus has a long url on the Internet which is a bit difficult to memorize. http://www.cs.wayne.edu/~kjz/ lampsacus/.

Some day there will also be a second, real city of that name on the globe - "as a site you can touch" -. Soon so many persons will owe so much to the home town of all persons on the Internet - where all information requirements are fulfilled for free - that they will wish to drive there in huge numbers with their families in order to be able to touch Lampsacus as a real city. In this place that has not been determined yet and which will be ready to assume the role of ancient Lampsacus in reality you will find - as on the Internet - a Multicultural Society of Minorities (MSM). I.e. a society where different nationalities with their cultures and traditions will live and act together with other minority groups (such as obese people, lesbians, mentally ill, disabled, poor people, etc) and not against each other.

POSSIBILITIES OF REALISING L+MSM

The paragraph above sounded like a page from a prospectus for the Riviera. But everybody knows: there is no such thing as a "free lunch": Nobody will pay for your lunch without no strings attached. So where's the sting in the tail, or even the fraud?

So instead of going into raptures over the unique opportunities that Lampsacus offers to us (with the largest library, the largest university and the largest newspaper and the largest post-office of the world) we would rather do it "the other way round". Anybody who wishes to do so, can change from the camp of timid pessimist to the camp of future-oriented optimists. How? By thinking independently through all the oh-so-reasonable objections raised to Lampsacus, and maybe by even turning them around autonomously in his or her mind. For one will find one's own opinion only on the basis of a mature judgement. It helps a lot if all the counter-arguments are already on hand.

Indeed, scepticism of the readers cannot be large enough. Apart from promises you will not find anything else on the Internet site. Promises, however, are cheap, because they do not cost money. Thus money will become - as is so often the case - once again a fundamental problem, at least this seems to be the case, or not? No, as an exception to the rule there is a different problem this time. What is missing is a nation. Yes, this does not have anything to do with the "friendliest nation" (as Nicolas Negroponte calls the Internet users), what is missing is a host nation. For even the most well-meaning institutions of the world, the planned L+MSM (Lampsacus and the Multicultural Society of Minorities) need a sponsor so as to become reality. Incidentally, also a small country is suited for this purpose. There is, however, one problem: This country would have to be incurably optimistic. The rolling stone thus could have struck itself. Have we cut the ground from under our feet? Is a real nation feasible after all?

There is a long tradition in a country of this world which makes it the ideal future host. However, if we simply stated the name of this country this might impair its ability to take this decision. For this reason, we cannot reveal its name. Conversely this also entails the risk that this country might miss the historic opportunity.

Nothing is so difficult to predict as the future. The development of the Internet and everything related to it is very fast-moving. We see a Multicultural Society of Minorities appearing on the horizon via a second Internet (Lampsacus) - like the sun lingering above the sea. Is there a possibility to grasp it like a mirage with a zoom lens or even like a non-utopia that can be realised already now?

FINANCING OF LAMPSACUS

Lampsacus is extremely labour-intensive. The numerous jobs that it creates have to be secured - at least for the circle of permanent employees - with a foundation. Which size does the foundation have to have in order to guarantee that the project can continue on its own once it has been started?

We believe that once funding has been secured that Lampsacus will see the light of the day. We were asked whether a small start would be better than no start. The answer seems to be no. 200 years ago a free-of-charge mail service for the entire planet only could have been established if a financially powerful fund had been founded with the assignment of making the impossible possible. We are thinking of an endowment fund of 10 Billion Dollars out of whose interest income an annual one billion dollars would be available for the creation and financing of employees, satellites and the acquired programmes.

Apart from the money problem, we are facing a logistical problem which is the fact that what we regard as the overheating of the high-performance engine of "progress" will remain digital within in the foreseeable future. Owing to the digital revolution, production is faster than consumption, thus automatically creating more leisure time, which, in turn, will result in the generation of less social welfare benefits. For this reason it would be sensible to use part of our leisure time for our fellow human beings; particularly in the industrialised countries, however, this must be regarded as not realisable.

It is unavoidable that the society of Lampsacus will adapt to the continuous technical and digitised progress, for instance, via reductions of working hours or more part-time work. After all, like hard consumer goods, theoretical knowledge can be produced more rapidly than it is sold, or to put it differently, it is possible to produce much more than there is money or customers. It is only through distribution without charge that "progress via progress" is generated which will re-establish healthy economic growth for all. This means that economic progress presupposes progress in terms of information (that is free of charge). Lampsacus facilitates the surmounting of this global bottleneck.

This leads us to the burning question as to how many jobs Lampsacus will create?

Our answer to this question is: that it is simply not possible to predict in an age of technical and social changes taking place at breakneck speed whether 30000, 100000 or even millions of new jobs will be created. After all, this depends, as was already mentioned, on the framework conditions. For instance, with a 25-hour-week less new jobs are created and maintained than with 50 working hours per week. By the same token, the number of created jobs depends on the amount of holidays an employee enjoys per year and the duration of life hours of work. Nevertheless we are able to reduce this to a formula, even though we are no economists. The longer the hours that people work, the higher the unemployment rate. In order to combat this development, socially acceptable framework conditions need to be created by politicians, employers and unions. This is, at any rate, the opinion of French Socialist politicians. We believe that there is a foreseeable solution. We see that free access to information for all will create, first of all, the largest service company in the world, and secondly, will facilitate the access to and the creation of new jobs for a huge number of persons.

WHEN WILL LAMPSACUS BE REALISED?

It is an open question, when Lampsacus will be realised. it is even more questionable, whether it can become such a "brave" new reality with the qualities of a MSM. It is certain, however, that it is possible. Many things that became reality in the past were rejected at first, because they represented danger, for instance, the radio, cinema, TV, video, letterpress printing, computer, CD, down to the railway and space travel. It is probably better not to repeat the initial concerns in detail. After all, this book intends to give new insights as to whether L+MSM is to become reality. Are we already beginning Lampsacus in some spheres of life or are we maybe even right in the middle of it already?

IS PROFIT A MUST?

As early as in the time of the ancient Romans and Greeks people wanted to make profit. To this end they exploited their slaves and did not shy a away from wars in order to "bring peace" to their neighbours. Some people claim that profit and the greed for ever more wealth were the demise not only of ancient Rome and before that of ancient Greece, but also of several well-known and unknown small empires and social systems. In those days the world had not become a global village yet so that it was still easy to find an excuse for wars. Can Lampsacus make globalisation and peace possible, something that everybody is constantly spouting about, but that is actually in no way realised?

Is Lampsacus doomed to fail due to half-hearted practice as did past utopias? Although Lampsacus is not a utopia - for utopias are dependent on technical and moral developments that have not taken place yet - we still have to see to it that this plant is not destroyed due to the greed of individuals or a whole group before it actually is able to grow.

Even though Lampsacus is only an artificial world as yet, the following question is justified: is profit really a must? We will come back to that question. The word Internet was still a foreign word at the beginning of the nineties, however, by the end of the nineties, the Internet developed so rapidly that even computer experts were amazed.
In spite of its low costs the Internet is laid out as a market characterised by capitalism promising huge profits in the long-term. It is thus comprehensible that many parties try to get money out of the Internet users. Social concerns and particularly social action simply drop out. One gains the impression that a market economy resting entirely on capitalism, on the one hand, and social co-

existence, on the other hand, are incompatible. In Europe people are searching for a compromise that is to make the impossible possible. Is Lampsacus the solution?

In order to meet the danger of a social collapse everybody is called upon to take part in Lampsacus. This is possible now. One can create autonomous towns and countries with computer games which are positively or negatively influenced and modified by the correct decisions taken by the individual players.

It is certain for the authors, however, that Lampsacus will also be a game in the beginning, for not only children learn things playfully for real life, but also adults. Yet soon the games will be over, as L+MSM can be realised in the present, i.e. in the near future. The preconditions for this purpose have never been better. By interconnecting the personal computers in increasingly more households throughout the world, the Internet will be extended gradually at a global level. This means that persons in every corner of the world will be able to communicate at any time.

L+MSM inside and outside the Internet does not intend to make real profit, rather it regards the amalgamation of all peoples, with the maintenance of their cultures and traditions, without exploitation by modern slavery, as far as progress allows this independently from Lampsacus, as its profit. This does not mean, however, that the introduction of Lampsacus would not create a huge number of jobs and thus would boost the economy to an undreamt-of extent. Of course, the generated economic boom can be seen, if you like, as "profit".

PART II POWER AND MEDIA

WILL THE POWERS THAT BE ALLOW LAMPSACUS

When implementing a new social order it is justified to ask whether the powers that be will allow this or whether it is just a dream that the media can make a difference?

As the powers that be and the media are closely intertwined, because the mass media are used by the powers that be and the media makers come to power also via the media, the readers will ask themselves which interest the powers that be could have in Lampsacus? As L+MSM does not aim at any material profit most of the high and mighty should hardly show any interest. As there is profit in material terms, even though the result is an invaluable gain as peoples grow together, pacifism becomes a matter of course, and world peace will be attainable, the high and mighty will release the Internet for the realisation of Lampsacus. But that is not all yet, there is even the possibility that they will support it with every available means. If Lampsacus changes the power structure of the world, the powers that be inevitably will have to deal with it.

This sounds very nice, one should keep in mind, however, that this is not the whole picture. There will always be war-mongers, and what is even worse, they will not be interested in Lampsacus. As it might even pose a threat for them, they will attempt to fight Lampsacus precisely because of its idealistic benefits. L+MSM is thus no panacea for peace, but in any case it will contribute to the creation of a global community of nations. The goal of harmonious neighbourhoods will reduce wars and preserve material goods. Lampsacus will thus become a tremendous gain for humankind.

DOES HUMANKIND ALLOW IT?

Twenty points of criticism can be voiced levelled at the new possibility of harmonious neighborhood on the Internet, called Lampsacus.

We will simply enumerate them and would be grateful if you, as readers, could give us your opinion when you find this pamphlet in your post box, on the street, on the Internet or in this book.

Maybe you even wish to compile a COUNTER-LIST? Please do so, but first of all our list of counter-arguments will follow:

TWENTY HYPOTHESES AGAINST LAMPSACUS

<u>1.</u> "The sponsoring country will exert too much influence."

The country sponsoring Lampsacus and MSM would command such a level of influence that this would lead to a bias on the planet. That would be undemocratic.

<u>2.</u> "Cultural colonialism practiced by the sponsoring country."
Cultural colonialism would be inevitable, and this risk remains even if "<u>the transnational Democracy</u>" (Lampsacus) were allowed to set up its own rules (as planned, including an equal "right to visibility" for all cultures).

<u>3.</u> "Destabilization of the Planet."
The access to any desired piece of information for every inhabitant of the earth, and the access to the software market granted to each inhabitant by their home town on free visits are a curse and blessing at once: Everybody obtains a carte blanche to a "future life", but whether it is put to meaningful use without a destabilizing effect remains an unanswered question.

<u>4.</u> "Change in the general attitude towards "work""
The tremendous number of new jobs – created first in the sponsoring country and then everywhere else - is opposed to today's widespread conviction that work is a "valuable asset" that requires "rationing".

<u>5.</u> "It is more noble to wait and make losses."
Lampsacus and MSM require many satellites and the world's most user-friendly software in order to ensure equal access for grandma and her grandchild. Instead of requesting quotations by means of a competition it is better to wait until Bill Gates has to rent the satellites.

6. "A rational approach is useful only in road traffic."
We can hardly feel the traditional optimism of science any more as it is such a long time ago that innovations were produced in Europe. The rationalistic belief in progress is a thing of an era long past in Europe – one might think.

7. "The overly harmomious atmosphere in Lampsacus is childish."
It is in fact almost impossible to offer and maintain a clean place to live and to work for everybody. This is indeed more like a Disneyland fantasy. It could be a good idea to offer a competition on how one could keep Lampsacus clean and functioning while keeping traffic rules at a minimum. Is that, however, too rationalistic a thought?

8. "Science for all strengthens mainly the weak."
Perhaps the high state of science that will be fostered at the educational institutions of Lampsacus (Earth-Moon University, Sun School) should not be established or maintained in the first place, because, in an era without an arms race every future progress in science will inevitably be more likely to benefit those that are still weak today, not those who used to be strong. Lowering the prices for AIDS medication will have little impact on the "First World", but a tremendous impact on the "Third World". Lampsacus is similar and that is also true for science as a whole.

9. "Danger of encouraging emancipation."
In addition, the rationalism of science is dangerous as it confirms Gandhi's hypothesis that the origin of strength is not the group but anxiety-free dignity of the individual, that is stronger than an Empire.

10. "Exporting rationalism represents a threat to values."
It is well-known that rationalism only deals with shadows, the quantitative accuracy of the world. Qualitative aspects remain a blind spot. This means that moral values are compromised. This objection to Descartes is still relevant today.

11. "The Enlightenment has been refuted by physics."
Since its discovery, quantum mechanics has allegedly proven rational (local) models of the world wrong. Exporting a science that has refuted rationalism seems doubtful.

12. "Science improves the self-feeling of the young."
Perhaps young people – who are our future – should not be informed too explicitly of their own importance, as there are – relatively speaking – significantly less young people in the traditional cradles of science than on the remaining planet.

13. "The 6-billion-Grizzlies hypothesis."
A well-known biologist has claimed recently that the planet would not be able to sustain 6 billion Grizzly bears either. This sounds like a call for "planetary cleansing" and should better be kept a secret. The danger of a second Holocaust is growing, unless we conceal from the young people in the world the danger they are in. It might therefore make sense to put the antidote – Lampsacus - under a taboo as well. For historic experience shows that risks are growing the more you are looking for rescue. The best-known counterexampls are Gorbatschow and Mandela. However, both gentlemen's achievements have not earned final recognition yet. Lampsacus would be the third example in this series. Would that be desirable?

14. "The worldwide underrating of science would be curbed."
Scientists themselves have proved that they are no longer needed, since their status declined while their protest was scarcely worth mentioning. After we were flooded with scientists from the former Eastern Block, it was mainly junior positions that have been cut with irreparable consequences. Lampsacus would be capable of reversing this trend.

15. "According to a widespread opinion, evolution is something which cannot be predicted nor controlled."
The Internet enables a new evolution, which is said to be just as unpredictable as the biological evolution. Lampsacus and the Multicultural Society of Minorities claim, however, that they respond to an already recognisable "attractor of the future", and, in fact, anticipate it.

16. "Lampsacus is too fascinating to be allowed."
For everything that is fun must be forbidden.

17. "The English language would become a Lingua Franca – a generally known language - just like in Roman times."
On the globe, English is merely a minority language. Even if Lampsacus was to be reflected in all languages, English would be favored.

18. "Wait and see."
The market will make it by itself one day and demonstrate, whether L+MSM make sense or not.

19. "Human rights for every human being? "
According to the opinion of many humans (leaving aside some idealists and scientists), human rights depend on the culture.

20. "The project of becoming a person in Lampsacus goes too far."

Artifical persons - based on other kinds of animals or computers – are ethically problematic, as is the new Turing Test that was invented for them. Nevertheless we intend to use them as subjects for research at the Earth Moon University of Lampsacus.

WHY 20 COUNTER-HYPOTHESES?

These were the twenty hypotheses speaking against Lampsacus and MSM. This approach seems rather dangerous, since the authors believe that the correct answer is in fact the opposite of what is claimed above. Nevertheless they (we) were courageous enough to pay lipservice to a widespread opinion and to leave it up to our readers to decide where they stand.

Conducting such an experiment with the readers may be something which is only possible in a European country, because, firstly, people here are more self-oppinionated and critical than elsewhere. Secondly, we believe, the only chance to find a majority here is by being as sceptical as possible in our arguments – as we attempted to do above. This might seem cynical, however, we do not mean it this way. For the natural opposite of widespread scepticism is – to our mind – a greater willingness to take decisions independently and to carry out these decisions. It is therefore the most effective strategy to make oneself absolutely vulnerable. Whatever escapes cynicism can grow in Europe. This gives rise to the question of whether Lampsacus is capable of escaping cynicism successfully?

It was a trivial mistake that Chess World Champion Casparov committed when playing against "Deep Blue", the dark blue IBM computer, that led to his defeat. This was the surprising conclusion of a 14-year old from Tübingen, Germany. The hope that impenetrable clouds may be parted by a single ray of sun light, is something which is typical of children and dreamers, but sometimes adults are also allowed to talk like this.

To be explicit, we regard all 20 hypotheses listed above as wrong, in fact inherently fascistic. Nevertheless, we take the necessary debate seriously. The entailed risk is that, if only a few citizens manage to see through these transparent counter-hypotheses and recognize the correct future perspective and get to like it, there might not be enough time left for this place on the globe to implement the necessary renewal to a large extent. Some day, the future will arrive here, too. But we simply do not believe that such a delay is necessary. What do you say?

OPPORTUNITIES FOR THE INDUSTRIALIZED COUNTRIES

A short while ago we heard somebody asking the following question: "What was the use of all the development aid we paid apart from increased competition on world markets?"

If asked like that, the question gives rise to the conclusion that the industrialized countries are in fact hardly interested in seriously promoting education and know-how in the Third World. Rather, their intention seems to be to keep the working population of the Third World dependent to such an extent that it cannot become autonomous at all or become serious competition for their promoters and maybe one day to squeeze them out of world markets. After all, no small business man in a town would give a chance to a smaller or larger competitor in the same town facing bankruptcy, for instance, the healthy company passing on some extra orders to the ailing company. This would constitute social behaviour, but liberal market economy would not allow such behaviour according to the traditional view. So the stronger business man will stand by and watch the very livelihood of the competitor melt away, while his own monopoly grows and consolidates.

Such behaviour, however, is not envisaged in Lampsacus, the Multicultural Society of Minorities. And this is precisely the opportunity for industrialised countries. Is this not a contradiction?

Is it realistic to try to create a world market in which it is possible to get rich without exploiting others or starving them to death, no matter where they might live on the earth? Making this dream come true and testing it for its feasibility is something that is possible today via the Internet: Still, hardly anybody can believe that it will come true, even though everybody feels it would actually be the better solution.

For example, already today architects or programmers in India have the same opportunities as their competitors from the industrialised countries to access the Internet to offer their knowledge and work on the network of data highways. This way, our fellow earth citizens are enabled to raise their standard of living, which, in turn, raises their life expectancy. On the other hand, their colleagues in the industrialised countries are encouraged, already today, to cooperate more closely and more socially with their competitors from the Third World - to the benefit of both sides.

However, as it exists, this situation has already become fragile. The enormous purchase prices and upgrade costs (system updates on the PC to make soft- and hardware more compatible with the Internet) are the reason why thus far only a relatively small privileged group is able to benefit from the advantages mentioned above in the Third World, and also in what used to be the "Second World". The rest of the population is facing enormous difficulties in keeping pace with the future-oriented development, or in participating in it at all. Unnecessary social hot-spots are emerging here and, in addition, a lot of good knowledge and hard work is getting lost, jeopardizing world peace in the long term and leading to reduced profits everywhere. After all, one market is always better than no market.

It would therefore be generally desirable to make state-of-the-art technologies available at all schools and colleges in the world in order to enable all earth dwellers to participate in progress and to contribute to shaping the world.

However, until this can be the case, the industrialized countries have the possibility and the task to distribute the huge commercial market of the Internet in an appropriate and fair way. The idea behind Lampsacus deserves to be explored more profoundly and helped to mature. Should Lampsacus be helped to mature or is the dream that we mentioned an illusion?

OPPORTUNITIES FOR THE THIRD WORLD

In the previous chapter we mentioned some of the advantages afforded to the Third World by Lampsacus+MSM.

BENEFITS FOR DEMOCRACY

Apart from the stated threats to democracy (such as power abuse) there are also nearly unbelievable advantages for democracy.

The second author of this book had a first-hand experience of this benefit. When the state publicly exerted pressure on him and his wife (after both of them obtained professorships alien to their main research subjects – an unprecedented case) by having their apartment opened by force and committing Otto Rössler to an institution, he found support on the Internet in 1995. Within a short period of time he received an international declaration of solidarity made by 196 colleagues from throughout the world. An American colleague had started a „Cry for Help for Family Rössler" from the USA. To date it is unique in the history of the Internet and in the history of the 20th century that someone received so much support from his colleagues via a new medium, and what is more within only 2 days.

For this reason the Internet may indeed ensure democracy. Lampsacus+MSM are not only an attempt to pay back the good that has been done but also the attempt to make this experience part of every one's human rights.

The basic suitability of the Internet for such possibilities is also illustrated by the well-known creation of spontaneous opinions and the possibility of conducting plebiscites on political decisions or even polls as to whether this or that new product will really fulfil the promises that were given in the commercials.
Such representative opinions can develop within a breath-takingly short period of time, even though several million of people from all over the world participate in the process, which would have been either impossible without the Internet or realisable only with

huge financial means. You as readers, however, will have to find out whether this is in the interest of centralised power structures, or not.

Be that as is may, for the authors it is quite clear that L+MSM are social, democratic, humane, international, and global. Above all, however, for the country that establishes Lampsacus, it is the key to a golden future. Never before was it possible for a small country to be mentioned in future history books by carrying out a small investment. Strangely enough this altruistic act is at the same time the door to an unprecedented economic and human development.

In order to help L+MSM progress involving all earth dwellers, it would, for example, be desirable by all means to avoid a development of the Internet in a form which helps a few to secure for themselves an anti-social and unfair monopoly. Hard- and software markets should not be outdated already after 3 years. Lampsacus would take on the function of an international standard on the Internet in its area, allowing all countries to afford making investments in the future.

Information technology will not only change our lives in an economic respect, it will also change the lives of the people in the second and Third World.

This will lead to profound changes as they manifest themselves in the industrialised countries already today. Old job profiles and markets will become superfluous and new job profiles and markets will emerge. A new international standard will establish itself within the next 10-20 years.

Lampsacus can help to make this new standard come true swiftly to the benefit of all earth citizens. L+MSM can ensure that the time needed for transition will be as short, as humane and as socially sustainable as possible. That, however, requires politicians and companies to endorse the citizens' democratic desire to set up Lampsacus. This, in turn, presupposes that such democratic desire arises in the first place. To which extent does this democratic desire exist? It is the purpose of this book to try to provide the basis to answer this question.

CAN LAMPSACUS MAKE DEMOCRACIES GROW TOGETHER?

Can the Internet amalgamate the peoples on earth? Can Lampsacus amalgamate the peoples to become a Multicultural Society of Minorities? The experiment has not been carried out yet. There is no time frame yet for carrying it out. In fact, we believe that Lampsacus+MSM will be the challenge of the next century.

It is also clear, however, that Lampsacus cannot be a panacea and, just like any other social system before it, once established, it will not remain forever. Lampsacus is about offering the opportunity to all peoples in the world to come together as equal partners in an emerging world democracy. At present, the Internet is ideal for that purpose.

Are we right? Is Lampsacus something positive? The reader has realised that we expect something previously unheard of from Lampsacus, something we could call global brotherhood. Such a brotherhood would be as useful for the future, as is the peaceful neighbourhood of Tübingen and Reutlingen (two towns which used to wage war against each other only until a few hundred years ago) which we take for granted today. However, this book was not written out of idealism. It originates from the egotism of the principle of market economy. Establishing Lampsacus, the Multicultural Society of Minorities, is big business representing a safe investment in the future and provides a maximum of jobs at minimum costs. The country, offering home as a livelihood will become the home town on the Internet for all people. Is that Idealism or outright egotism? Strangely enough this is one of the rare questions that allows for both answers.

PART 3 - LAMPSACUS WORLD

USING LAMPSACUS

How will Lampsacus be used? The authors have no user manual ready yet, because although some approaches embracing L+MSM do already exist in the world, it is still theory which needs to be put into practice.

We would be pleased to see our small booklet familiarize as many people on the blue planet as possible with Lampsacus - it is sprung from Chaos. It will be thanks to your initiative that we may soon hold a manual on Lampsacus in our hands, which can then be refined by all of us in a common effort. Then there might be a chance that Lampsacus will not be overwhelmed by the spinning wheels of time as fast as other social developments have been.

WHERE DOES LAMPSACUS EXIST?

Lampsacus is not meant to exist exclusively on the Internet, but in reality, just like "Disney World", however, entirely realistic and true-to-life. With one exception: Disney World was there first, and followed by the Internet, of which Walt Disney Corporation benefits in line with the principles of free market economy.

The Internet, on which Lampsacus can be achieved and set up, is already in existence. For the first time, the human right to information, knowledge and education can be guaranteed - through Lampsacus. Lampsacus will form the second, free of charge Internet, that can be used by everybody - rich and poor. It will be like the telephone that has become a part of ordinary life in most parts of the world, but free of charge (and for local phone calls this has been the case for decades in large parts of America). People, who have a phone and pay a monthly fee should be entitled to use it, without having to pay more. The same is true for cable TV. Wherever such infrastructure does not exist, or where people want access to Lampsacus, without the two amenities (telephone, TV), the access is to be provided free of charge: with the help of the free satellite service of Lampsacus.

It is, above all in the villages in poor countries, where people cannot afford cable access for their young people, that the devices should be provided including the necessary dish. This is no illusion. It is not more of a revolutionary idea than the seemingly maniac suggestion of undertaking huge efforts to build roads and aqueducts (long-distance water pipelines) in Roman times.

Just like highways and schools are not unselfish gifts given by the state to the population, Lampsacus will become the lifeblood of a global society, which it won't be able to do without after a very short time.

Of course we would also like to encourage the reader to participate in the shaping of Lampsacus, the Multicultural Society of Minorities. We would therefore like to ask you to look for a location for Lampsacus and help to set it up.

DRAWBACKS FOR DEMOCRACY ?

Further above we have stated, that Lampsacus will bring about real democracy. Already today, the Internet is, as mentioned above, the "friendliest nation". Since the beginning of humankind, democracy is what it is all about. The understanding of concepts favoured today - democracy, human dignity and free market economy - differs everywhere. And apart from these desirable possibilities there are far less desirable systems like dictatorships. In view of the insufficiency of the world there is, of course, also the danger of the abusing the Internet and therefore also L+MSM. Therefore, we have to make sure, for example, that individual countries and regional communities like Europe do not become too dependent on the Internet.

It is true that the Internet could be sabotaged by undemocratic governments. It could, for example, be abused by undemocratic governments as an information source for the dissemination of falsified information. By means of a monopolized Internet, the population could be fooled, because the Internet will soon acquire the same importance as other media. But the Internet could also be used by terrorist groups for acts of sabotage. To put it in simple terms, the possibilities of abusing the Internet seem almost unlimited.

A second point: computers and the Internet also bring about the danger of the absolutely "see-through" human being. Compared to such a scenario, Orwell's 1984 would be one of many special offers in an overcrowded department store shelf. Such concerns can be derived from the current progress of the world of computers. As we all know, banks and advertising agencies have become almost perfect in analysing the buying behaviour of individual consumer groups or even the individual consumer. Employers are able to portrait their individual employees in quite a comprehensive way, even when it comes to their private lives.

Therefore, there will be the Lampsacus secret analogous to the secrecy of the post. Lampsacus will, as we have said, become something like the "second post office". Everybody can use the postal service as well as the huge information service that it offers free of charge. Now that the post office and its services are progressively privatised, and the idea of the "service to the citizen" (as originally developed by R. Hill) is more and more forgotten, Lampsacus wants to give rise to the idea of making life easier for all people once again.

The Authors

Wilfried Kriese was born in 1963 and was trainedas a carpenter. Since 1989 he is a workman at the University of Tübingen. He made a name for himself as writer and publisher for minorities after publishing to date 14 books which deal mainly with minority and social issues. Since 1984 he has been involved in politics for directly affected minorities in the political party "Die Grünen". After standing candidate for a mandate (once at a regional and twice at a national level) Wilfried Kriese is the first person with a past learning disorder in Germany that applied for such mandates. In view of the fact that there are approximately 1 million persons in Germany living with a learning disorder, this might set us thinking, as it proves how difficult it is to break out of the pre-determined restrictions that are set for minorities.

Otto E. Rössler, born 1940, holds the title of a medical doctor and gives lectures at the University of Tübingen as Professor for Biochemistry (voluntarily) and as Professor for Chemistry (involuntarily). Throughout the world he is one of the most respected researchers of Chaos Theory.
As three police operations in the lecture theatre did not dissuade him from exercising his right of free speech he has become famous beyond the scientific circle and across Europe's borders. Today Otto E. Rössler is one of the best-known figures of the University of Tübingen since its existence.